Saving Petey

A Prairie Dog's Journey

Maureen Lawry

Copyright © Maureen Lawry, 2025
All Rights Reserved

This book is subject to the condition that no part of this book is to be reproduced, transmitted in any form or means; electronic or mechanical, stored in a retrieval system, photocopied, recorded, scanned, or otherwise. Any of these actions require the proper written permission of the author.

This is a story about...

The children at Mountain Shadows School,

who come face to face with a serious problem in their schoolyard: prairie dogs have moved in! Petey, a delightful little prairie dog, and his coterie* faced a big issue in their new home. The land is being overrun by children playing.

AND

The gardener, Mr. Boots, was concerned that the same land was unsafe for both the children and the prairie dogs.

"Is there a way to settle this and make both the prairie dogs and the school happy?", he wondered.

One day, the children noticed many little mounds all over their playground.

Curious little Pippa asked, "How did they get here? Are they important?"

Mr. Boots, the gardener, panicked and exclaimed, "Aaaaaak, Yikes, prairie dogs on the playground! No! Sound the alarm! They all must go! Call the police, call Maureen, call an ambulance! CALL SOMEONE!"

Pippa thoughtfully calmed Mr. Boots, saying, "Maybe we can explore ways to solve this problem."

Mr. Boots yelled, "They are all bad, and I KNOW we can't share the playground! They will make us all get sick! They could bite us!" Mr. Boots ran in circles, screaming, "NO!, NO!"

After a bit of "digging" in their library, the children decided they needed to teach Mr. Boots what they learned about prairie dogs.

"Mr. Boots listened as they explained that prairie dogs play a big role in helping at least 124 other species survive. Prairie dogs are an important food source for many predators, and their burrows are used by reptiles, birds, insects, and other mammals as cozy homes or hiding places."

"What? How can this be true? They are Bad! They are BAD! BAD! BAD!" yelled Mr. Boots.

Pippa explained, "Prairie dogs are a Keystone Species*, you are worrying about MYTHS! Keystone Species, like the prairie dogs, are heroes of the animal kingdom! They hold everything together."

"Hmmmm," thought Mr. Boots. "Can this be true? Can the ecosystem begin to collapse? Will other species disappear without prairie dogs?"

The keystone is the stone at the top of an arch that holds everything together. Without it, the whole arch could collapse.

Prairie dogs are the keystone species of the grassland ecosystem.

"Let's look at how prairie dogs are vital to the survival of several mammals," said Pippa.

"Hey, Petey! My name is Carl, the coyote. I am looking for a friend to invite to my house for lunch. Why don't you come? I'd love to have a prairie dog for lunch!"

"Oh yes, Carl, I love making new friends! Let me ask my Grandmother! " Petey enthusiastically said.

"Petey, NO, NO! Why not surprise your Granny AFTER we eat our lunch? Come on with me, my new little friend, we can…" Carl was interrupted as all the prairie dogs on the playground began to yip and call!

"Oh, Carl! There is danger in the prairie dog town! Come with me to my burrow…QUICK! QUICK, "screamed Petey as he jumped into the safety of his home.

"Well, drat," said Carl. **"I am the danger**, and now I won't have a yummy prairie dog for my lunch. Those prairie dogs and their warning calls ruined my lunch!"

Fun Fact: Prairie dogs talk to each other. Their many squeaks are just like our words. They can warn other prairie dogs about danger. They have a special sound for each predator.

Now said Pippa,"Let's look at another mammal, the bison."

Petey gasped as he looked at the HUGE animal.

"This must be a dragon or maybe even a monster!"

"Well, hi there, little guy. My name is Tatanka.* I am a bison and love eating in prairie dog towns."

"YIKES!" Petey was terrified the bison was going to eat him!

"Don't be scared, Petey; we eat grasses and naturally coexist*. We like that you keep the grass short and sweet for us."

"Well, that's a relief," said Petey.

"It looks like you stay close to all your enormous friends, Tatanka."

"Oh yes, Petey, We are prey, just like you and your family. And just like you, we stay close together to protect each other."

"WHAT? YOU are prey? Who are your predators, monsters?"

Fun Fact: Bison are the largest land animal in North America. They weigh more than 2000 pounds and run 35 miles per hour, but wolf packs will prey on the weak members in the herd. Their defense is staying close together.

Pippa was still learning about the prairie. "Now, let's check out the birds that benefit from prairie dog."

"Hey, little owl, I'm Petey; why do you like to live in prairie dog burrows?"

"Hoot, Hoot. Hi, Petey. You have created a nice, comfy burrow to live in and have the same predators as owls. We listen for your warning calls, which also keep us safe!"

"Yes, but it's daytime, don't owls hunt at night?"

"Not burrowing owls. We hunt insects during the day, and we have a very clever way to attract insects."

Petey was curious, "What is that?"

"We cover our nests with excrement….you know, dung….manure?"

"WHAT? You catch insects with POOP?" Yuck! Petey couldn't believe his ears!!

Fun Facts: Burrowing owls rely on other animal burrows, like the prairie dog burrow, for a home. Did you know that young burrowing owls make a sound like rattlesnakes to scare away predators when their parents are away? It keeps them safe. It's one of their defenses.

"Mr. Boots, do you see that beautiful bird in the sky? That is a Ferruginous Hawk! That's the biggest of all of the hawks. Their main food source is prairie dogs," Pippa explained. "Prairie dogs are an important food source for birds of prey like hawks and eagles."

"I can hear the other prairie dogs' warning calls, but I want to look at this beautiful bird. I don't want to go into the burrow," exclaimed Petey as he settled back to look at the hawk.

"FURR—-EW—GIN—OUS!" Petey laughs as he says the funny name.

"FURR—-EW—GIN—OUS!

FURR—-EW—GIN—OUS!"

"Get into your burrow! You need to stay safe!" call all the other prairie dogs. But they continued to hear…..

"Furr—-ew—gin—ous!……..Furr—-ew—gin—ous!…Furr—-ew—gin—ous!"

From deeper and deeper in the burrow.

Fun Fact: The ferruginous hawk has feathered legs all the way down to its toes, a rare trait among hawks that's more typical of birds adapted to cold climates, like the golden eagle. These leg feathers help protect it while nesting on the open prairie, where it faces cold winds and little cover. It is also the biggest hawk in North America.

"Let's check out reptiles in the prairie dog town." Pippa is still doing her research!

SSSSSSS.............SSSSSSSS......SSSSSSSSSS..

The snake hissed as he slithered into the burrow.

Petey knew it was his turn to warn his friends of the danger! Petey sounded the warning call for the snake. This told the prairie dogs to get out of their tunnels. Then Petey and his friends pushed the dirt into the burrow to trap the snake. A prairie dog system has many entrances and exits. Petey's family members can get out and are safe.

Fun Fact: It's the only venomous snake native to the Northern Plains. It's rattle is made of Keratin, like your fingernails. They give birth to live young. They are shy and like to be left alone. They can hear with their jaws!!

Fun Fact: Harvester ants are known for their potent venom and are considered one of the most toxic insects in the world.

Let's look at another reptile:

"Hey, look, this piece of bark is moving!" said Petey, curiously checking out another entrance to his burrow.

"No, no, I am not a piece of bark. I am a horned lizard, and I am looking for harvester ants for my lunch."

"I live in prairie dog burrows because I can take refuge there to escape predators and extreme temperatures if it gets too hot or cold for me—and I can be near my prey!"

Fun Fact: Horned lizards boast excellent camouflage. They have armored, spiky skin and can inflate their bodies to double their size. They squirt blood out of their eyes and can hit a target accurately at up to 5 feet!

Still another reptile:

"Hi, Turtle, what are YOU doing in the prairie dog town?"

"Well, hi, there," said the friendly little turtle, "I noticed a dung beetle running across the field, and I just love to eat dung beetles."

"Oh drat!" Turtle exclaimed, "He is so quick! He just ran down into your burrow, Petey. But that won't stop me! I'm going in after him!"

"Aaaah! Help! Help! I'm stuck! I CAN dig my way out, but it's gonna take a while…..and double drat, that dung beetle got away."

Fun Fact: The Plains Painted Turtle has a superpower, it can breathe through its bottom! When it's hiding under frozen water in winter, it doesn't need to come up for air. Instead, it soaks up oxygen through its bum.

Now let's look at the insects that live on the prairie.

Petey noticed some more dung beetles busily plodding through the grasses. Petey was curious. "Why are you in the prairie dog town?"

"Hi, Friend" said one little dung beetle. "We are collecting excrement and rolling it into balls."

"WHAT? You're collecting POOP?! You roll it into BALLS?! That is GROSS!! Why would you do that?!"

"Minerals in the dung or poop have important nutrients* we need. We also lay our eggs in the dung to keep them safe and warm until they hatch."

Fun Fact: Dung beetles are incredibly strong for their size. When the dung beetles are rolling the balls of dung, they can pull a whopping 1141 times their body weight - that's the same as you pulling six busses along a road!

Mr. Boots remarked, "I do see that prairie dogs are important and help so many animals. I do not want the ecosystem to begin to collapse, but they cannot be here on a playground where children play. They simply can not."

Pippa said, "There must be some way we can help our friends find a safe place to live."

Soon Pippa discovered the solution!

"I found out about a town called Pueblo that wants prairie dogs to come to their town! They are rebuilding the prairie ecosystem!"

But how do you get them there??

Lindsey Sterling Krank and her team from the Humane Society have relocated entire prairie dog towns. They will teach the children the best way to move the prairie dogs.

Soon, there were dozens of traps all over the playground.

"Gradually introducing prairie dogs to the traps will help them when it comes time for their big move, "explained Lindsey.

"Look!! The children have put seeds and peanut butter in these traps. I like going in and out daily to get my treats." Petey and his friends were excited about their new find.

Pippa knew winter was coming, and it was important to set the traps and move the critters to their new homes.

Joni told Maureen, "Let's take the prairie dogs to Pueblo soon so they can settle in before the winter."

Pueblo was their new forever home, where their deep burrows would help aerate the soil, manage water drainage, and help the many species of reptiles, birds, insects, and other mammals reestablish balance in this prairie ecosystem.

Thanks to the creative efforts of some curious, sweet, sensible and smart little children, Petey and his family are living happily in Pueblo on 23,000 acres of land! There is room for all the mammals, reptiles, insects, and birds to thrive. And there are no school playgrounds with little feet or Big Boots to bother them.

Fun Fact: The children of Mountain Shadows School want everyone to know that once considered extinct, the black-footed ferret has been discovered and is now repopulating in this Pueblo area. Colorado prairies with healthy prairie dog populations have played a big part in the black-footed ferret reintroduction.

Glossary

Aerate means to let air into something, like soil or water. Imagine you have a garden, and the soil is too tight for the plants to breathe. Aerating the soil helps by making holes in it so that air, water, and nutrients can get to the roots of the plants. This makes the plants healthier and stronger.

Coexist: means living together in the same place without hurting each other or causing problems. In this way, everyone can be happy and safe.

Coterie: is a special group of prairie dogs that live together in a small area. It's like a family! A coterie usually has one dad prairie dog, a few mom prairie dogs, and their babies.

Keystone Species are unique animals or plants that help keep their homes, or ecosystems, healthy and balanced. They are like superheroes because they do important jobs that help many other animals and plants survive. Even if there aren't many, they make a big difference.

Myths are stories or beliefs not based on facts but often passed down through generations. When presented as factual information, myths can contribute to the spread of misinformation.

Many people have heard the myth that prairie dogs carry the plague, but this is a misunderstanding of how the disease works. The truth is, prairie dogs don't carry the plague—the fleas do.

Species: a way to group living things that are very similar and can have babies together. Imagine all the dogs in the world; they are one species because they can have puppies together. Cats are another species because they can have kittens together, but dogs and cats can't have babies together. This helps us understand how different animals are related and how they fit into the world.

Tatanka: This is a Lakota word that means "buffalo," a significant animal in Native American culture, particularly among the Lakota people.

Water drainage: When prairie dogs dig their burrows, they help water drain into the ground. This prevents water from running off the surface and causing erosion by letting it flow deeper into the earth.

FUN FACT: (not really fun!)

When plague-carrying fleas find their way into a prairie dog colony, it's catastrophic for the animals. These colonies are susceptible to the disease, and entire populations can be wiped out within 24 to 48 hours of exposure. So, instead of being dangerous carriers, prairie dogs are plague victims.

So the next time someone mentions prairie dogs and plague in the same breath, you can gently set the record straight: it's the fleas, not the prairie dogs, and these fascinating little animals deserve protection, not blame.

mason.mc

JORDAN F.

ARTHUR F.

Luna.B

Molly Sh.

Winston W

Theo. T

Dahlia J

BEAR D
Wilder D

Ella.S.B

camille.P

Gideon
Julian B

theo.W

sanaa P.

Kiyandi K.

Maureen and Joni are on their way to Pueblo with Petey and his coterie.

Petey is plump and healthy and ready for his new home.

BIO

Maureen Lawry is an AMI-trained Montessori teacher, puppeteer, and lifelong educator based in the foothills of Boulder, where she lives with her husband, Dan. She honed her puppetry skills through a Fulbright Scholarship in Budapest and later developed a prairie-themed puppet show while serving as education chair of the Boulder Audubon Society with Mary Balzer. The show traveled to four states, bringing its stories to national parks, schools, and libraries—though it was once banned at a ranch school! Maureen has dedicated her career to connecting children with the natural world. She enjoys hiking, gardening, and buying too many art supplies.

Acknowledgments

Any book is the result of the efforts of many people. I want to thank my husband, Dan, who patiently listened to countless ideas and revisions. Your computer skills made this possible!

I am grateful to all the friends who brainstormed and read the many iterations of this work. You know who you are! Thank you to Karen Peterson, who came to the rescue when I ran in circles like Mr. Boots and yelled," Help."

I would also like to extend my heartfelt thanks to Lindsey Sterling Krank from the Humane Society and her team of experts for their help in relocating the prairie dogs.

A huge thank you to Joni Perry and her elementary students for their enthusiasm for learning about the grassland prairie ecosystem. Your curiosity and questions helped shape this book and reminded me why sharing knowledge with young minds is important.

Finally, I sincerely thank the prairie's wonder, resilience, and quiet beauty. Lastly, I want to thank the young readers whose curiosity and joy inspire me to write. This book is for you.

I appreciate the extra mile that Idris Matthews and Jonathan Parks from Panda Publishing Agency went to make this book happen on time,

  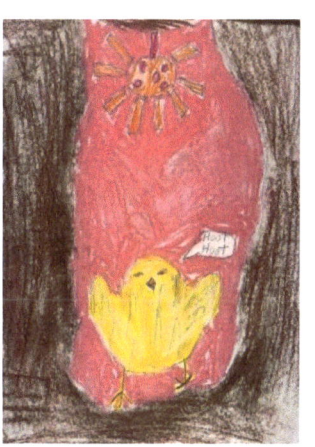

Dedication

To the children who stood up for the prairie dogs— You asked questions, took action, and showed the world that even the tiniest creatures deserve a home. Your kindness, courage, and determination inspire hope for the wild places and all who call them home. This book is for you.

www.ingramcontent.com/pod-product-compliance
Lightning Source LLC
Chambersburg PA
CBHW041104070526
44583CB00002B/46